Library of
Davidson College

NEW YEATS PAPERS VIII

*I hail the superhuman;
I call it death-in-life and life-in-death.*
                    W. B. Yeats, 'Byzantium', *ll.* 15-16

# DEATH-IN-LIFE AND LIFE-IN-DEATH: 'CUCHULAIN COMFORTED' AND 'NEWS FOR THE DELPHIC ORACLE'
BY KATHLEEN RAINE

THE DOLMEN PRESS

CONTENTS

| | |
|---|---|
| Cuchulain Comforted *by* W. B. Yeats | page 7 |
| News for the Delphic Oracle *by* W. B. Yeats | 8 |
| Death-in-Life and Life-in-Death | 11 |
| Note on *The Death of Cuchulain* | 55 |
| Notes on the Text | 57 |
| Acknowledgements | 61 |
| List of Illustrations | 61 |

General Editor: Liam Miller

This paper is a development of a lecture delivered to the Yeats International Summer School at Sligo, on 24 August 1972.

© 1974 Kathleen Raine
ISBN 0 85105 245 2

Printed and published in the Republic of Ireland at the Dolmen Press, North Richmond Industrial Estate, North Richmond Street, Dublin 1. First published in 1974.
Distributed outside Ireland, except in the United States of America and in Canada, by Oxford University Press.
Distributed in the United States of America and in Canada by Humanities Press Inc., 171 First Avenue, Atlantic Highlands, N.J. 07716.

1. The 'veiled' Goddess: Juno Samia Selenitis; engraving from Jacob Bryant's *New System of Mythology*, vol. 2 (1774), Plate vii.

# W. B. YEATS

## CUCHULAIN COMFORTED

A man that had six mortal wounds, a man
Violent and famous, strode among the dead;
Eyes stared out of the branches and were gone.

Then certain Shrouds that muttered head to head
Came and were gone. He leant upon a tree
As though to meditate on wounds and blood.

A Shroud that seemed to have authority
Among those bird-like things came, and let fall
A bundle of linen. Shrouds by two and three

Came creeping up because the man was still.
And thereupon that linen-carrier said:
'Your life can grow much sweeter if you will

'Obey our ancient rule and make a shroud;
Mainly because of what we only know
The rattle of those arms makes us afraid.

'We thread the needles' eyes, and all we do
All must together do.' That done, the man
Took up the nearest and began to sew.

'Now must we sing and sing the best we can,
But first you must be told our character:
Convicted cowards all, by kindred slain

'Or driven from home and left to die in fear.'
They sang, but had nor human tunes nor words,
Though all was done in common as before;

They had changed their throats and had the throats of birds.

### NEWS FOR THE DELPHIC ORACLE

I

There all the golden codgers lay,
There the silver dew,
And the great water sighed for love,
And the wind sighed too.
Man-picker Niamh leant and sighed
By Oisin on the grass;
There sighed amid his choir of love
Tall Pythagoras.
Plotinus came and looked about,
The salt-flakes on his breast,
And having stretched and yawned awhile
Lay sighing like the rest.

II

Straddling each a dolphin's back
And steadied by a fin,
Those Innocents re-live their death,
Their wounds open again.
The ecstatic waters laugh because
Their cries are sweet and strange,
Through their ancestral patterns dance,
And the brute dolphins plunge
Until, in some cliff-sheltered bay
Where wades the choir of love
Proffering its sacred laurel crowns,
They pitch their burdens off.

III

Slim adolescence that a nymph has stripped,
Peleus on Thetis stares.
Her limbs are delicate as an eyelid,
Love has blinded him with tears;
But Thetis' belly listens.
Down the mountain walls
From where Pan's cavern is
Intolerable music falls.
Foul goat-head, brutal arm appear,
Belly, shoulder, bum,
Flash fishlike; nymphs and satyrs
Copulate in the foam.

# DEATH-IN-LIFE AND LIFE-IN-DEATH

It was the fashion among my fellow-students at Cambridge in the late 'twenties to scoff at Yeats's interest in the 'mumbo-jumbo' (to use George Orwell's word) of what we dismissively called his 'occultism'. Our own complacency was of that unreasoning kind found in those who have never questioned the hidden premises of current opinion — in our own case the scientific view of 'reality'. Dr. I. A. Richards, himself the inventor of 'scientific' criticism, saw more clearly than did his students the magnitude of the issue when he wrote, in 1928, that 'the resort to trance and the effort to discover a new world-picture to replace that given by science, are the two most significant points for our purpose in Mr. Yeats's work.'[1] In 1936 R. P. Blackmur thought the subject of Yeats's magic worth a serious study; but expressed the general view when he wrote: 'the supernatural is simply not part of our mental furniture.'[2]

History is already beginning to reverse Blackmur's judgment. In a letter to Sturge Moore (27 May 1926) Yeats affirmed his belief that 'what Whitehead calls the "three provencial centuries" are over. Wisdom and poetry return.' Novelty is no merit in the eyes of the 'universal and unanimous tradition' of the Perennial Philosophy; and Yeats did not, any more than did Eliot whose ground was Christian theology, pretend to 'originality' in his metaphysics. His 'system' only looked novel to a generation ignorant of the depth and breadth of its foundations.

Irreconcilable with atheist humanism is the teaching that the soul is immortal; has existed before birth, and will continue after death. Virtually all the great works of human intellect and imagination prior to Whitehead's 'provincial centuries' have rested upon the knowledge of immortality. It must be obvious that the entire self-awareness of human beings must be different not only in certain respects and in certain situations, but in all respects and in every situation, according to whether the atheist or the traditional belief is held. And so also it must be with our ability to respond to every art in which mankind has expressed his natural and supernatural intuitions and aspirations.

Traditional poetry, learned or unlearned, is a language inseparable from those spiritual premises upon which it depends and from which its very terms are derived. It has this power fully only within the proper context of a traditional culture. When their universe of reference is unknown — or, as in the context of contemporary atheist humanism, denied outright — poetry and the other arts speak an obscure, and ultimately, a dead language. Yet the arts have in themselves a limited power of evoking and transmitting such knowledge, if not to the reason at least to the imagination. Is not the assent to Yeats's total vision the assent of intuitive self-knowledge to traditional themes, traditional images, and beyond these to the traditional metaphysics which informs his work? After the 'provincial centuries' he offers us, as does no other poet of this century, the norm, the measure of our humanity, the orientation of life and death within that whole, that One of which Plato and all the traditional philosophers speak.

Strangest of all to those conditioned by current materialist ideologies must be Yeats's preoccupation not with death as such but with that other life to which death is the gate. A sentimental and morbid preoccupation with physical death belongs to that humanism for which the death of the physical frame is the extinction of the being. For those who adhere to the universal tradition of the immortality of the soul the fact and manner of physical death recede into relative unimportance; or have an importance of a quite different kind. Speaking from his long experience Jung said that the psyche does not believe in death. Yeats from the beginning was seeking the traces of a doctrine, obscured by the provincial centuries, of the soul's history. The soul being immortal, the mystery of birth and death — so closely, so mysteriously related that Plato (quoting from Euripides[3]) asked 'who knows if life be death and death be life?'[4] — must be, within any traditional culture, for poet and philosopher, paramount. To say merely that he 'believed' in the soul's immortality is not even to indicate the complexity of Yeats's thought, the passion of his searchings for knowledge of the state of the discarnate. Yeats was no more troubled than was Blake with those 'doubts' so dear to agnostics. Not the fact, but the nature of our immortality, was his concern. The mortal man of atheist humanism is not merely in some, but in all respects a different being from Yeats's mysterious migrant who

2. The thirteenth Tarot Key: Death. From *The Twenty Two Keys of the Tarot* by Arland Ussher.

shudders in many cradles'. As he wrote to Olivia Shakespear (1 October 1932)[5]: 'only two topics can be of the least interest to a serious and studious mind — sex and the dead.' For generation and death are the gates between worlds. In a note (unpublished) on the Tarot Key of Death, Yeats wrote that the skeleton reaper goes accompanied by the symbolic figure of a new-born child; because for every death from one world there is a birth into another.

Reincarnation is an aspect of the universal doctrine upon which Christianity has frowned; though early Christian converts from Hellenism would have found nothing in the new teaching to contradict the old. If it is necessary to discover reasons why so deeply religious a poet as Yeats could not accept the Christian Church, was he not too deeply committed to the doctrine of rebirth? From all his chosen teachers — from Swedenborg and Blake, from the Fairy faith of Ireland's 'book of the people', from the theosophy and the Cabbalistic studies of the Order of the Golden Dawn, from Plato and Plotinus and 'out of a medium's mouth', from the Noh plays of Japan and the Tibean *Book of the Dead*, to the Vedas, Yeats gathered all the knowledge he could of the soul's history, of that hidden phase of our single human experience which follows death and precedes birth.

In the *Phaedo*[6] Socrates is described as passing the last hours of his own mortal life in discoursing upon the soul's coming and going between its two worlds or states, in an endless cycle of descent and return:

> Do you not admit that death is the opposite of life?
> I do.
> And that they come from one another?
> Yes.

Then what comes from the living?
The dead.
And what, asked Socrates, comes from the dead?
I must admit, he said, that it is the living.
So it is from the dead, Cebes, that living things and people come?
Evidently.
Then our souls do exist in the next world.
So it seems.

— and so to the conclusion that there must be an opposite process to that of dying, which can only be 'coming to life again'. Yeats in his own last poetic declaration of faith, 'Under Ben Bulben' is indeed following Socrates:

> Many times man lives and dies
> Between his two eternities,
> That of race and that of soul,
> And ancient Ireland knew it all.
>
> *ll.* 13-16

Ancient, not Catholic Ireland; for the allusion is to the doctrine of rebirth, implicit, so Yeats believed, in the 'fairy faith' as it had been in the teaching of the Druids.

Plato in the *Phaedo* makes Socrates say that 'true philosophers make dying their profession' because the philosopher 'will never attain to wisdom worthy of the name elsewhere than in the next world'[7]; only death frees the soul from contact with the body and its desires, which obscures the soul's innate wisdom. There follows Socrates' great discourse on the immortality of the soul; since death is the opposite of life, 'they come from one another, and have their two processes of generation between the two of them';[8] or as Yeats develops that thought,

> For wisdom is the property of the dead,
> A something incompatible with life; and power,
> Like everything that has the stain of blood,
> A property of the living.[9]

According to Swedenborg — and his teaching is supported by the evidence of modern spiritualism — the dead have access to the whole memory-record of a life-time, and must read and evaluate that record. This may be one sense in which we are to read Yeats's words, 'wisdom is the property of the dead'. But Plato's anamnesis seems to attribute to the discarnate another and deeper kind of knowledge. In several of the Platonic Dialogues it is argued that all knowledge is recollection of what the soul knows, and that nothing can be taught but what is already latent in the mind itself. In the *Phaedo* Socrates relates anamnesis—recollection—to the soul's knowledge of another state. 'What we call learning is really just recollection', and 'what we recollect now we must have learned at some time before, which is impossible unless our souls existed somewhere before they entered this human shape. So in that way too it seems likely that the soul is immortal.'[10]

Yeats's early teacher, Blake, took from Plato his own account of poetic recollection:

> In my Brain are studies & Chambers fill'd with books and pictures of old, which I wrote and painted in ages of Eternity before my mortal life; & those works are the Delight & Study of Archangels.[11]

Blake makes Plato's thought more concrete — 'books and pictures'. Yeats makes it more abstract, when in *A Vision* (p. 54) he writes: 'I think Plato symbolises by the word "memory" a relation to the timeless.' This was the relation (with *spiritus mundi*, tir-na n-Óg, the collective unconscious, the Self of the Upanishads, or the world of the dead) that Yeats was for ever attempting, by magical invocation, through spiritualist mediumship, even, on at least one recorded occasion, by the use of drugs, to realize. Monk Gibbon has recorded a conversation in which Yeats said: 'Of course death is a great moment of illumination for every man.' This must be so if, as Platonists have believed, 'wisdom is the property of the dead'.[12]

Y. Evans-Wentz, years before his Tibetan scholarship made him famous, put forward in his first book, *The Fairy Faith in Celtic Countries* (1911), the view that the 'fairy faith', with its implicit assumption of rebirth, is not a popular invention but the last trace of religion of the Druids, whose Hyperborean priest Abaris gave instructions to Pythagoras himself. True or false, we must assume that this view was shared by Yeats, to whom the book is dedicated, and who was regarded as an authority by its author. Perhaps it was Yeats who suggested to Evans-Wentz the similarity of much fairy-lore to the happenings in spiritualist séances. Or both may have taken this view from Andrew Lang, who in (for example) his comment on Robert Kirk's *The Secret Commonwealth* (1893 edition) makes this comparison. (Evans Wentz studied under Lang at Oxford.) What both Yeats and Evans-Wentz believed is that the world of faery is the world of the dead; near to the human, — nearer, perhaps, than most of us care to know — at once beautiful and alluring, and inimical to our world. As the Greeks said of the immortals, 'they live our death and die our life', so the country people believed that 'you may hear the newly-dropped lambs of faery crying in November . . . our spring being their autumn, our winter their summer'.[13] He appended an essay on 'Swedenborg, Mediums and the Desolate Places' (dated 1914) to Lady Gregory's *Visions and Beliefs in the West of Ireland* (1920) in which he wrote, (of the fairy faith):

> I had noticed many analogies in modern spiritism and began a more careful comparison, going a good deal to séances for the first time and reading all writers of any reputation I could find in English or French. . . . I did not go there for evidence of the kind the Society for Psychical Research would value any more than I would seek it in Galway or in Aran, I was comparing one form of belief with another, and like Paracelsus, who claimed to have collected his knowledge from midwife and hangman, I was discovering a philosophy.[14]

The time of which Yeats here writes is 'some fifteen years ago' — that is, before 1900. Then, he tells, one day he opened the *Spiritual Diary* of Swedenborg, which twenty years before he had 'read with some care before the fascination of Blake and Boehme had led me away.' (p. 297). The first reading of Swedenborg must have been, therefore, about 1880, almost in boyhood; and we may name Swedenborg as Yeats's earliest source of precise information about the state of the dead. In Swedenborg he believed he had found the same doctrine and practice 'of the desolate places, of shepherds and of midwives, and discovered a world of spirits, where there was a scenery like that of earth, human forms, grotesque or beautiful, senses that knew pleasure or pain, marriage and war.' (p. 298). It was from Swedenborg that Yeats took the belief that just as we create the places of our own dreams, so are our surroundings in the next world created by human imagination. In 'The Tower' he wrote:

> Death and life were not
> Till man made up the whole
> Lock, stock and barrel
> Out of his bitter soul,
> Aye, sun and moon and star, all.
> And further add to that
> That, being dead, we rise,
> Dream and so create
> Translunar Paradise.
>
> *ll.* 149-157

Swedenborg says that the appearances of things, in the world of the dead, are plastic to the thoughts and states of mind of the spirits; not 'fixed and dead' as in this world, but ever-changing, like dream images. 'So heaven and hell are built always anew and in hell or heaven all what they please and all are surrounded by scenes and circumstances which are the expression of their natures and the creation of their thought.[15] So it is in faery, whose people are shape-changers and illusionists. 'This earth-resembling life is the creation of the image-making power of the mind, plucked naked from the body, and mainly of the images in the memory.' (pp. 300-301).

Swedenborg had anticipated 'a discovery one had thought peculiar to the last generation' (possibly Yeats had Janet in mind) that the 'most minute particulars which enter the memory remain there and are never obliterated'.[16] So the world of the dead is at first 'like the unfolding of a dream' of past life. 'But gradually we begin to change and possess only those memories we have related to our emotion or our thought; all that was accidental or habitual dies away and we begin an active present life', in which 'the ruling love has begun to remake circumstances and our body.' (p. 302).

How much of Swedenborg's thought is there in 'The Phases of the Moon', and the souls in flight from dreams 'Crying to one another like bats' like the shades of the Homeric suitors of Penelope who

> ... speak what's blown into the mind,
> Deformed beyond deformity, unformed,
> Insipid as the dough before it's baked,
> They change their bodies at a word.
>
> *ll.* 110-113

Such are the apparitions at a séance, the illusions cast by witches, the phantasamagoria of faery, the 'heavens' and 'hells' of Swedenborg built by 'correspondence' to thought.

Yeats first used the image of the dough in his essay on Swedenborg. Telling how discarnate spirits are made anew in accordance with their 'ruling love', he writes that if we were to meet our friends 'now for the first time we should not recognise them, for all has been kneaded up anew'. He then quotes Swedenborg: Every man has many loves, but still they have reference to his ruling love, and make one with it, or together compose it.'[17] In 'The Phases of the Moon' Robartes uses the same phrase:

> When all the dough has been so kneaded up
> That it can take what form cook Nature fancies. . . .
>
> *ll.* 114-115

The process of incarnation is itself seen by Yeats (on the authority of Porphyry's *De Antro Nympharum*) as a process of materialization or 'condensation' of a body about some airy spirit. 'Souls who love the body attach a moist spirit to them and condense it like a cloud' (p. 329) shaping 'that mysterious substance, which may be life itself'.[18]

In the essay on Swedenborg Yeats describes the flight of the dead seeking what is related to their ruling love:

> During the rending and fusing man flits, as it were, from one flock of the dead to another, seeking always those who are like himself, for as he puts off disguise he becomes unable to endure what is unrelated to his love, even becoming insane among things that are too fine for him.[19]

Yeats goes on to describe how the philosophy of Swedenborg was adapted to 'the séance room'. Modern books on spiritualism tend always to assume that the heavens and hells of the discarnate are self-created, and none of these eternal. These scenes are built up to a great extent from the memories of earthly life, only gradually changing as the discarnate spirits, in a world as busy as ours, begin to re-form both themselves and their surroundings.

In the same essay on Swedenborg[20] and again in 'The Soul in Judgment' section of *A Vision*[21] Yeats describes the plots of Japanese *Noh* plays, whose theme is often some fantasy of earthbound spirits; like that of *Motome-Zuka*, the fantasy of the earthbound ghost of a young girl who had caused the death of a mandarin duck, shot by her two competing lovers. 'The priest tells her that if she can but cease to believe in her punishments they will cease to exist. She listens in gratitude but she cannot cease to believe.' (p. 339). Yeats's own spirit-plays, *Words Upon the Window-pane* and *Purgatory* describe spirits caught up in the memories of some passionate moment of life.

In 'Shepherd and Goatherd' the reversal of time in the 'dreaming back' leads to the 'dayspring of life; a concept Yeats again learned from Swedenborg:

> Jaunting, journeying
> To his own dayspring
> He unpacks the loaded pern
> Of all 'twas pain and joy to learn,
> Of all that he had made.
>
> *ll.* 98-102

The 'dayspring' also recalls Plato's famous myth in the *Politicus* which tells how, whereas now we move from youth to age, in the 'golden age' of Saturn the journey is reversed, and men move from age to youth. The 'loaded pern' too is Platonic, and recalls the Three Fates who, in *The Republic* (Book X) spin, measure, and cut the thread of life:

> Who talks of Plato's spindle,
> What set it whirling round?
> Eternity may dwindle,
> Time is unwound.
>
> 'The Bargain', *ll.* 1-4

Eternity 'dwindles' as time is unwound into the life-story of this world; a process reversed in the 'dreaming back' of the dead as they remember their earthly lives in reverse order.

As he grew older and more learned in traditional knowledge, Yeats moved from a predominantly experimental to an increasingly metaphysical approach to 'the Beyond'; from the techniques of magic, the collecting of folk lore, and after *A Vision*, even from mediumship, to the Platonic philosophers, and above all Plotinus. Yet the premise of all these studies, from first to last, the experience of the soul as it comes and goes between two worlds, remains unchanged. There is no abandonment of the earlier beliefs but an entirely consistent development. It is natural that experiment should have preceded metaphysics; and doubtless Yeats came to Plotinus because in him more than in any other philosopher he discovered a cosmology, a metaphysics, consistent with the nature of man as he had come to understand it. The fourth *Ennead* ('On the Soul') is of the essence of Yeats's life-long preoccupation with the nature and destiny of the soul, his realization that the whole of human experience must include the discarnate no less than the incarnate, death and life as inseparably part of what we are at all times. Only Dante and Blake have so laboured to restore that lost fullness of the experience of what we are as did Yeats. In the *Noh* plays of Japan he found an art-form based upon the interrelation of the living and the dead; in Plotinus a philosophy.

Yeats's greatest poems on the soul, on rebirth, on the relation between the experience of the temporal and of the eternal, were written after a late and mature reading — or rereading after he had written *A Vision*, as he tells us, — of Mackenna's Plotinus. It is especially in the fourth *Ennead*, 'On the Soul', that we find traces of Yeats's mind passing over Mackenna's pages. Here as elsewhere, the unanimity of Tradition may mislead us; Blake, for example, was saturated in Plotinus, and in particular the tractate (which he knew in Thomas Taylor's translation) 'On the Descent of the Soul'.

The phrase 'The soul recovers radical innocence' ('A Prayer for my Daughter', 1920) can be understood in the light of *Ennead* IV, from such passages as:

> The soul has lost that innocency of conducting the higher which it knew when it stood in the All-soul . . . but in spite of this it has, for ever, something transcendent: by a conversion towards the intellectual act, it is loosed from its shackles and soars — when only it makes its memories the starting point of a new vision of essential being.[22]

'The Phases of the Moon' (published in 1919), with its summary of the soul's history as it completes its cycles of rebirth, has, (even though Yeats tells us that his systematic reading of Mackenna's Plotinus was after finishing *A Vision* (1927) echoes of the same Ennead; when we read

> The soul, remembering its loneliness
> Shudders in many cradles
>
> *ll.* 91-92

the soul's 'loneliness' recalls Plotinus' 'the flight of the alone to the Alone'.[23] The 'cradles' are surely too close for the resemblance to be coincidental to this description of the descending souls making their way:

> each to a very place of its own . . . it is a partial thing isolated, weakened, full of care, [the soul] intent upon the fragment, severed from the whole, it nestles in one form of being; for this, it abandons all else.[24]

The phrase 'the crime of death and birth', which is the theme of 'A Dialogue of Self and Soul' is nearer to Plotinus than to Plato; even though Plotinus takes Plato as his authority for regarding a 'descent' into incarnation as a 'crime' of the generating soul; for Plato in his fable of the Cave speaks of the generated soul as fettered in darkness; and in the *Phaedrus* speaks of the soul losing its wings as it approaches the body. 'In all these explanations he finds guilt at the arrival of soul at the body.' Yet Plotinus also says — and in this Yeats followed him — that

> It is possible to reconcile all these apparent contradictions — the divine sowing to birth, as opposed to a voluntary descent aiming at the completion of the universe; the judgment and the cave; necessity and free choice — in face the necessity includes

the choice — embodiment as an evil; the Empodoclean teaching of a flight from God, a wandering away, a sin, bringing its punishment; the "solace by flight" of Heraklitus; in a word voluntary descent which is also involuntary.[25]

It may be that Yeats found the 'solace by flight' in Heraklitus, but, associated as it is with so much that Plotinus has also taught, we might be tempted to guess that it was from him that Yeats learned the teaching of Michael Robartes:

> Reformer, merchant, statesman, learned man,
> Dutiful husband, honest wife by turn,
> Cradle upon cradle and all in flight, and all
> Deformed because there's no deformity
> But saves us from a dream.
>
> *ll.* 101-105

In two late poems Yeats deeply considers the discarnate state and its relation to this life. In 'Cuchulain Comforted' the poet imagines the soul of the newly-dead hero on its first arrival among the shades; and in Yeats, no less than in Dante and in Virgil himself, it is the belief of the poet in the reality of that situation as a part of the human experience that makes his words not fanciful but 'tongued with fire'. In 'News for the Delphic Oracle' (a more fanciful poem, whose tone of irony is nevertheless merely the vesture of Yeats's veritably religious theme), another hero — or the same hero under another name — is to be born; and the poem describes the longing for rebirth into this world. The poem is dated 13 January 1939; on 28 January he died. A few days before he had read to Lady Dorothy Wellesley the prose theme of the poem:

> A shade recently arrived went through a valley in the Country of the Dead; he had six mortal wounds, but had been a tall, strong, handsome man. Other shades looked at him from among the trees. Sometimes they went near to him and then went away quickly. At last he sat down, he seemed very tired. Gradually the shades gathered round him, and one of them who seemed to have some authority among the others laid a parcel of linen at his feet. One of the others said: "I am not so afraid of him now that he is sitting still. It was the way his arms

rattled." Then another shade said: "You would be much more comfortable if you would make a shroud and wear it instead of the arms. We have brought you some linen. If you make it yourself you will be much happier, but of course we will thread the needles. We do everything together, so everyone of us will thread a needle, so when we have laid them at your feet you will take whichever you like best." The man with the six wounds saw that nobody had ever threaded needles so swiftly and so smoothly. He took the threaded needles and began to sew, and one of the shades said: "We will sing to you while you sew; but you will like to know who we are. We are the people who run away from the battles. Some of us have been put to death as cowards, but others have hidden, and some even died without people knowing they were cowards." Then they began to sing, and they did not sing like men and women, but like linnets that had been stood on a perch and taught by a good singing master.[26]

The poem, written as the poet was nearing his own death, must have at its core an irreducible mystery which relates to his own experience of that approach; so long a theme of speculation, but now entered upon as a reality.

The figure of Cuchulain, the Irish Hercules, is Yeats himself; a strange identification of the poet with his anti-self, the hero. Cuchulain had long accompanied Yeats's poetic thought, and the identification with Hercules is his own. In the (unpublished) General Introduction to his work, written in 1937, two years before the writing of the poem, he describes the Republican hero Pearse, who 'went out to die calling upon Cuchulain:

> Fall, Hercules, from Heaven in tempests hurled
> To cleanse the beastly stable of the world.'[27]

Here the association seems to be purely heroic, as in the lines from 'The Statues':

> When Pearse summoned Cuchulain to his side
> What stalked through the Post Office?
>
> ll. 25-26

But the fable of Hercules among the shades had long been associated in Yeats's mind with his own spiritualist studies. In 1914 he concluded his essay on Swedenborg with an allusion to that passage in the Odyssey

> where Odysseus speaks not with "the mighty Heracles", but with his phantom, for he himself "hath joy at the banquet among the deathless gods and hath to wife Hebe of the fair ankles, child of Zeus, and Hera of the golden sandals," while all about the phantom "there was a clamour of the dead, as it were fowls flying everywhere in fear and he, like black night and with bow uncased, and shaft upon the string, fiercely glancing around like one in the act to shoot." [28]

The striding figure of Cuchulain suggests too that other 'violent and famous' hero among the shade, the Homeric Achilles who in the Odyssey 'strode' away from Odysseus. The figure of Yeats's Cuchulain, who

> ... leant upon a tree
> as though to meditate on wounds and blood
>
> *ll. 5-6*

is close to those Greek heroic shades who, like so many spirits described by Swedenborg (and perhaps those young soldiers of the first World War described in spiritualist works of the time and well known to Yeats) seem not to know they are dead and continue after death in the activities and thoughts of the last moments on earth. The eyes that 'stared out of the branches and were gone' suggest Homer's dead, 'as it were fowls flying everywhere in fear'.

The souls of the dead have been likened to birds from time immemorial; the *Ka* spirits of ancient Egypt are depicted as birds; the slain suitors of Penelope; the white birds of Ireland and the other Celtic countries. Long before Yeats had written in *The Shadowy Waters*:

> ... Gull, gannet, or diver,
> But with a man's head, or a fair woman's,
> They hover over the masthead awhile
> To wait their friends; but when their friends have come
> They'll fly upon that secret way of theirs ...

3. Cuchulain: Statue by Oliver Sheppard in the General Post Office, Dublin. The Morrigu in bird-form is perched above the head of the hero, who is bound with the 'veil', as described by Yeats in *The Death of Cuchulain*.

These birds are the souls of the dead:

> ... There's one of them that says
> "How light we are, now we are changed to birds!"
> Another answers, "Maybe we shall find
> Our heart's desire now that we are so light."
> And then one asks another how he died,
> And says, "A sword-blade pierced me in my sleep"
> And now they all wheel suddenly and fly ...[29]

4. The Morrigu. Mask designed by Liam Miller and Hugh Kearns for a production at the Lantern Theatre, Dublin, 1972.

In an early version of *The Shadowy Waters* Forgael is haunted by more terrible eagle-headed beings.

In 1939 Yeats wrote his last play, *The Death of Cuchulain*. In this play the Morrigu, the Irish Valkyrie, gatherer of slain heroes, appears in her bird-form; not a white bird, but the black raven, that bird who throughout north-western Europe is a portent of death. The goddess enters and stands, invisible, between the *fey* Cuchulain and his last love, Eithne Inguba. Eithne becomes aware of her:

EITHNE   I know that somebody or something is there,
         Yet nobody that I can see.
CUCHULAIN              There is nobody
EITHNE   Who among the gods of the air and upper air
         Has a bird's head?
CUCHULAIN                 Morrigu is headed like a crow.
EITHNE (*dazed*)  Morrigu, war-goddess, stands between.
         Her black wing touched me upon the shoulder, and
         All is intelligible.         (*The Morrigu goes out*)
                     Maeve put me in a trance.
         Though when Cuchulain slept with her as a boy
         She seemed as pretty as a bird, she has changed,
         She has an eye in the middle of her forehead.

5. Cloth by Edmund Dulac for the first production of *At the Hawk's Well*, 1916.

The allusion to the earlier encounter is to *The Hawk's Well*, in which the goddess is hawk formed.

Later, wounded and awaiting his death, in a passage that recalls *The Shadowy Waters*, Cuchulain seems to himself about to assume the bird-form of the dead:

> . . . there floats out there
> The shape that I shall take when I am dead,
> My soul's first shape, a soft feathery shape,
> And is it not a strange shape for the soul
> Of a great fighting man?

In 'The Soul in Judgment' section of *A Vision*[30] Yeats again returned to the Homeric image of Heracles. The angry phantom is

> . . . compelled to live over and over again the events that had moved it. . . . They occur in the order of their intensity or luminosity, the more intense first, and the painful are commonly the more intense, and repeat themselves again and again. . . . All that keeps the *Spirit* from its freedom may be compared to a

> knot that has to be untied or to an oscillation or a violence that must end in a return to equilibrium. I think of the Homeric contrast between Heracles passing through the night, bow in hand, and Heracles, the freed spirit, a happy god among the gods.

He then quotes in William Morris's translation the lines describing Heracles at the feast of the Gods (quoted on p. 24). Plotinus uses the same myth.[31] It seems unlikely that Yeats's attention had not been caught by at least this passage in Mackenna's Plotinus before he wrote *A Vision*, the theme of the soul's history, and the very myth Plotinus takes as his illustration having for so long been part of his own thought. He had certainly read it before the writing of 'Cuchulain Comforted'. Plotinus sees the 'shade' of the hero as what Yeats calls (in contrast to the soul) the 'self':

> ... thus it is that the shade of Hercules in the lower regions — this "shade", as I take it, being the characteristically human part — remembers all the action and experience of life, since that career was mainly of the hero's own personal shaping.

Blake also distinguished between 'the spectre' or 'the shadowy man' and 'the true man'; he too taking the terms from Plotinus, and Yeats from both.

In his essay on 'Swedenborg, Mediums, and the Desolate Places' Yeats had described the boats and horses and weapons buried by the ancient Egyptians with their dead. These, he suggests, 'were helps for a flagging memory or a too weak fancy to imagine and so substantiate the old surroundings'.[32] The body of an apparition was held to be 'a brief, artificial dreamy, half-living thing', a body 'contrived' from its memories; and the allusion to Heracles, as already quoted, follows. But in contrast to the Egyptians who seemingly sought to reactivate earthly memories, Plotinus holds that 'the good soul is the forgetful';[33] and again it is the Homeric Hercules he takes for example:

> The Hercules of the heavenly regions would still tell of his feats. But there is the other man to whom all that is trivial; he has been translated to a holier place; he has won his way to the Intellectual Realm.

(The term 'heaven' is here used of that intermediate state of which Swedenborg and the spiritualists have written so much.)

Cuchulain's fantasy of wounds, blood and the rattle of arms that makes the dead afraid proves the dead hero to be, in the words of Plotinus, 'still dragged a captive', unable to free himself of the experiences of his recent life; like the heroine of the Noh play *Motome-Zuka*, who relives her story, unable to realize that her hells of punishment are a self-created, self-inflicted fantasy.

Who are the 'certain Shrouds that muttered head to head', of such dignity that Yeats capitalizes the initial letter? They are intimately related to the hero in the moment of his death, but in what way we are not told, and the emotion of fear they stir in us would not be so intense were their identity disclosed. The shroud is a commonplace in the Celtic world of second sight as a portent of death. Yeats possessed a copy of the 1933 edition (with commentary by Andrew Lang) of Kirk's *Secret Commonwealth*, where he would have read (if a literary source be required) in Lord Tarbett's Letter (appended to Kirk's text) giving an account of his own 'Inquiry', made in 1653, how Highland seers 'if they sie the Species of any Person who is sick to die, they sie them covered over with the shrowding Sheet'. (p. 93).

In the play *The Death of Cuchulain* (to which the poem is in some respects a postscript) the heads of the six slain men who had given the hero his mortal wounds are displayed by the Morrigu:

> This head is great Cuchulain's, those other six
> Gave him six mortal wounds . . .

— and each is described; some valiant, others of no account. The play concludes with the dance of Emer before the severed heads of Cuchulain himself and the six warriors who slew him. The seven dead warriors are united in the death they have shared.[34] Yet the Shrouds of the poem seem somewhat different in nature. They partake in that Platonic ambiguity of those who 'in the words of Heraclitus "live each other's death, die each other's life" '.[35] The first, most striking meaning, which has given these beings that awe-inspiring numinosity indicated by the capital letter, must be the poet's premonition of his own approaching death. It is 'Our graves that shroud us from the searching sun'; but the body is the shroud of

6. John Donne's monument in St. Pa[ul's] Cathedral, London. This sculpt[ure,] with its suggestion at once of de[ath] and resurrection, was made acc[ord]ing to the poet's own instructi[ons,] he himself standing in his shrou[d to] serve as the model of his own eff[igy.]

the soul in generation. There is a passage in the *Hermetica* which describes the body as

> the web of ignorance, the foundation of all Mischief; the bond of Corruption, the dark Coverture; the living Death; the sensible Carcass; the Sepulchre, carried about us . . . such is the hurtful Apparel, wherewith thou art clothed, which draws and pulls thee downward . . . thou shouldst hate the wickedness of this garment . . .[36]

This figure constantly appears in Gnostic texts. In 'The Soul in Judgment'[37] Yeats refers to the 'Hymn of the Soul' which his friend, G. R. S. Mead had translated, in which 'a King's son asleep in Egypt (physical life) is sent a cloak which is also an image of his body. He sets out to his father's kingdom wrapped in the cloak.'

The same concept of the mortal body assumed as a shroud by the soul as it 'descends' into this world is found in Blake's 'The Gates of Paradise (ed. Keynes, p. 771):

7. Blake: The worm (Blake's customary symbol of the mortal body) in her winding-sheet, in 'the regions of the grave'. *The Gates of Paradise*, plate 16.

I have said to the Worm Thou art my mother & my sister

When weary Man enters his Cave
He meets his Saviour in the Grave.

Some find a Female Garment there,
And some a Male, woven with care,

Lest the Sexual Garments sweet
Should grow a devouring Winding Sheet.

*ll.* 19-24

8. Blake: The generated soul woven into the 'filmy Woof', *Jerusalem* (1804-1820), Plate 37, detail.

This sinister animated garment is described in greater detail by Blake in *Vala* Night the First; a poem on which Yeats himself had spent so much thought as its first editor.[38] The Shrouds give advice to the hero which arouses, in the context of the poem, the thrill of terror we feel in certain dreams. First one 'let fall a bundle of linen'; and as they gather about him the insistence grows stronger:

And thereupon that linen-carrier said:
"Your life can grow much sweeter if you will
Obey our ancient rule and make a shroud."

*ll.* 11-13

That ambiguous advice warns the dreamer to prepare himself for the grave; but equally it tells of rebirth, of 'death-in-life and life-in-death', for as the dead are vested in a shroud, so are the newborn 'woven' into mortal garments.

The oldest literary source of this symbol is doubtless the Homeric cave-temple of the nymphs who weave the bodies of mortality upon stone looms — the bones, according to Porphyry's *De Antro Nympharum*, which both Yeats and Blake had read, and upon which both poets drew freely. For these symbols have a long history, and are inseparable from the philosophy which they illustrate. For poets who have placed themselves within this tradition there could be no apter symbol of the mortal body than the garment each soul must weave for itself in its 'descent' into generation.

Yeats's 'bundle of linen', therefore, is a compact allusion to this traditional symbol; but especially, perhaps, to Blake's 'stalks of flax' from which Enion spins the 'woof of terror' into which Tharmas, the eternal man' is woven, 'a pale white corse':

> He sunk down into the sea, a pale white corse:
> In torments he sunk down and flow'd among her filmy Woof.
> 
> *Vala* I, ll. 64-65

The 'filmy woof' is the mortal body, and this body has a life of its own:

> Wond'ring she [Enion] saw her woof begin to animate, & not
> As Garments woven subservient to her hands, but having a will
> Of its own, perverse & wayward . . .
> 
> *Vala* I, ll. 83-85

This mortal body, whose will opposes itself to the soul which is, according to the Hermetic and Platonic tradition, the true substance of the 'shadowy' reflection in matter, becomes, in Blake's mythology, Vala herself, who gives her name to his first long poem upon the descent and return of the soul. We remember also Coleridge's 'Life in Death', more sinister than Death himself with whom she plays dice for the souls of lost mariners sailing the 'sea of time and space'.

9. Blake: Vala (veiled) mother of mortal bodies, and Jerusalem (nude) mother of souls. *Jerusalem*, Plate 32.

The 'veil' of Vala (whose name is itself probably derived from the name of her chief attribute) is Blake's symbol of the natural body. Vala, the 'goddess Nature', is depicted as 'cruel' in her weaving of this veil, in which she catches the souls of mankind, weaving them into its texture, caught like fish in a net. It is most likely that Yeats in his play *The Death of Cuchulain* had in mind Vala's 'veil' of the physical body, which is both man's cradle and his shroud, when he makes Aoife, Cuchulain's old love, ceremonially bind him with her 'veil'. She appears, who was once beautiful, as bride and mother of his son, as the hag, the sinister aspect of the Triple Goddess in her office of the enshrouder of the dead:

10. *The Bride* by William Calvert. This line engraving, by one of that group of younger artists who took Blake as their master, is is within the iconographic tradition of the 'veiled' goddess from which Blake himself derived, and which he transmitted. Yeats greatly admired this engraving.

> AOIFE But I am an old woman now, and that
> Your strength may not start up when the time comes
> I wind my veil about this ancient stone
> And fasten you to it.

Cuchulain's reply is even more suggestive of Vala's 'veil' of nature, whose beauty Blake too describes in many passages:

> CUCHULAIN But do not spoil your veil.
> Your veils are beautiful, some with threads of gold.

(These 'veils' are of course physical bodies.)

> AOIFE I am too old to care for such things now.
> (*She has wound the veil about him*)
> CUCHULAIN There was no reason so to spoil your veil:

The death-hag cares no longer for those beautiful bodies of infancy and youth.

In this strange dialogue it is the mysterious resonance of the underlying myth of the 'veil' of the human body which the Triple Goddess both gives and takes away that gives it such power.

The Shrouds are, as it were, a collective being:

> ... and all we do
> All must together do."
> ll. 16-17

11. Blake: Design (early 1790's) for Gray's *The Fatal Sisters*.

Swedenborg's 'heavens' and 'hells' are peopled with group-souls, societies of souls in the same spiritual state; and Blake followed him when he wrote of those 'States'

> when distant they appear as One Man, but as you approach they appear Multitudes of Nations. . . . I have seen, when at a distance, Multitudes of Men in Harmony appear like a single Infant.[39]

In 'The Soul in Judgment' Yeats tells that 'some spirit once said to me: "we do nothing singly, every act is done by a number at the same instant." Their perfection is a shared purpose or idea.'[40]

Whether or not this explanation of these mysterious figures be the true one, they have affinity with Cuchulain as aspects of himself; and this makes the more remarkable their revelation of their nature:

> "But first you must be told our character:
> Convicted cowards all, by kinsmen slain
> Or driven from home and left to die in fear."
>
> ll. 20-22

In placing his epic hero among cowards is Yeats recalling Cornelius Agrippa on the 'laws of Adrastia'? It is likely that this is so; for in his essay on Swedenborg he had quoted from *De Occulta Philosophia* a passage on the fate of the evil dead, who see represented 'in the fantastic reason', as if in a dream, flames, drownings, evil beasts and other terrors. In the same short work there is a passage Yeats does not quote but which Blake made use of in his poem 'Tiriel'. Agrippa describes the fantasies of the dead as obeying a law of compensation, in which each must suffer from his own besetting sin, as did his victim. So kings and tyrants become slaves and are at the mercy of such as they themselves had been. In more sophisticated terms Yeats himself wrote:

> Those who inhabit the "unconscious mind" are the complement or opposite of mind's consciousness and are there . . . because of spiritual affinity or bonds created during past lives.[41]

The 'convicted cowards' are the hero's anti-self. The passage from Plotinus quoted above (IV, iii, 27) as related to the figure of Hercules, continues with an account of how the soul in its post-mortem stage begins to remember its former incarnations.

> The soul, still a dragged captive, will tell of all the man did and felt; but upon death there will appear as time passes memories of the lives lived before.

Are these elusive figures that approach the dead hero memories of former incarnations, of bodily shrouds worn by the soul in former lives? Plotinus describes (in Mackenna's phrase) 'soul-phases' lived in former incarnations. All these are in some sense one being:

> ... the other souls (soul-phases) going to constitute the joint-being could, for all their different standing, have nothing to recount but events of that same life, doings which they knew from the time of their association: perhaps they would add some moral judgment.   (IV, iii, 27)

12. Blake: Daughters of Los (Time) at the Wheel, spinning the 'fibres of life'.

Yeats's 'Shroud that seemed to have authority' might be one among these phases more significant than the rest. But this is speculation.

In a concentrated and splendid image the 'shrouds' themselves tell the hero, ' "we thread the needle's eyes" '. The shock and mystery come in part from the unexpectedness of such an image in the context of the death of the hero; and yet it is singularly appropriate on several levels. Lady Gregory in her *Cuchulain of Muirthemne*, described the 'nine feats' with which Cuchulain amused the women of Ulster:

And he took three times fifty needles from the women, and threw them up, one after the other, and in that way they were all joined together. Then he gave every woman her needle back into her own hand.

But the symbol carries the meaning far beyond the fantasy of the heroic feat. In the Gospel it is through the needle's eye that a man enters the Kingdom of Heaven. The image suggests also the narrow entrance of womb and passage-grave, the dimensionless *punctum* through which life comes or goes. Above all, the needle's eye is apt to receive the thread of destiny spun by the Fates that runs on 'Plato's spindle' from birth to death, and, in the 'dreaming back', when 'time is unwound' from death to birth.

> All the stream that's roaring by
> Came out of a needle's eye;
> Things unborn, things that are gone,
> From needle's eye still goad it on.
> ('A Needle's Eye')

13. The thread of Fate: detail from Blake's water-colour drawing illustrating Gray's *Ode on the Death of a Favourite Cat*. See also Plate .

14. Blake: The Blessed Virgin Mary drawing yarn from a distaff: Illustration (c. 1816) to Milton's *Paradise Regained*.

15. The Blessed Virgin Mary with spinning-wheel and distaff: detail from illustration to the *Divine Comedy* (1827) no. 3. In these two depictions of the symbolism of generation, Blake indicates that through the Christian Mystery of the Incarnation the 'body of death' is redeemed.

It is, in the prose summary, the shrouds who thread the needles; 'everyone of us will thread a needle, so when we have laid them at your feet you will take whichever you like best.' The souls Plato describes in the Tenth Book of the *Republic* as about to enter incarnation choose from many which lie scattered on the ground 'patterns of lives'; and the first man to choose 'at once sprang to seize the greatest tyranny'[42] 'without sufficient examination' as Plato says; and afterwards regrets his choice. 'The prophet placed the patterns of lives before them on the ground; far more numerous than the assembly. They were every variety. . . .' (X, a and b). Odysseus, who came last, took a long time to choose, being a cautious man. If Yeats had in mind this passage — and it would be virtually impossible for any traditional poet describing the mythology of rebirth not to think of Plato's parable — there is a grandeur of indifference in the hero's gesture who 'Took up the nearest and began to sew' (1. 18). In the poem there is no noun to which 'the nearest' is related; presumably to the threaded needles of the prose theme; which correspond, in the context, to Plato's 'patterns of lives':

> Your life can grow much sweeter if you will
> Obey our ancient rule and make a shroud;
> Mainly because of what we only know
> The rattle of those arms makes us afraid.
>
> *ll.* 12-15

In the prose draft there is the suggestion that 'easeful death' is sweeter than life, the shroud 'more comfortable' than the armour of the living, who must fight life's battle.

Is what makes the 'shrouds' afraid the 'phantom' still earthbound? Or is the hero warned that he can free himself from the obsession with his past life only by entering upon another?

> Cradle upon cradle and all in flight and all
> Deformed because there is no deformity
> But saves us from a dream.[43]

To the soul filled with passion and desire, to act is better than to dream. We know that Yeats himself chose — as in this poem the shrouds advise Cuchulain to choose — rebirth:

16. Blake: *The Gates of Paradise*, Frontispiece (1793). The crysalis with the face of a sleeping infant suggests at once the unborn child about to enter this life, and the 'body of death' awaiting metamorphosis.

17. Was Blake's image suggested by some such Tudor effigy as that of Robert Clayton, in St. Giles's Church, Ickenham, Middlesex, 'who dyed 16th of August 1665 within a few howres after his birth'

    (This effigy was reproduced on the title-page of a volume of poems by Frances Bellerby, published by the Enitharmon Press, London, 1970; to whom, and to Mrs. Bellerby, acknowledgements are made.)

> I am content to live it all again,
> And yet again, if it be life to pitch
> Into the frog-spawn of a blind man's ditch,
> A blind man battering blind men⁴⁴

— a battle, as for Cuchulain. Or in 'His Bargain', already quoted:

> However they may take it,
> Before the thread began
> I made, and may not break it
> When the last thread has run,
> A bargain with that hair
> And all the windings there.
>
> *ll.* 7-12

With masterly ambiguity 'that hair' is at once the thread of fate wound on Plato's spindle, threading the needle's eye, and the hair of the beloved which draws the lover back to incarnation, through desire, as in 'Mohini Chatterjee'.

> "Old lovers yet may have
> All that time denied —
> Grave is heaped on grave
> That they be satisfied —"
>
> *ll.* 17-20

In 'A Dialogue of Self and Soul' he claims '... as by a soldier's right / A charter to commit the crime once more' (ll. 31-32) — the Plotinian 'crime' of rebirth. The soldier, who embodies Ares, the principle of Strife which is, according to the Empedoclean teaching, the cause of the setting-going of the universe itself, is always, for Yeats, the type of generated existence; of 'a blind man battering blind men'. Sato's sword and its embroidered sheath are, he says, 'emblematical of love and war', the Empedoclean antinomies, Ares and Eros. 'The rattle of those arms' makes the shrouds afraid of Cuchulain's restless phantom fit only for rebirth. No detail of Yeats's mature symbolism is ever arbitrary; and if Plotinus swimming towards the isles of the blessed is the type of the man freed from generation, Cuchulain, Achilles, Heracles are, as embodiments of Discord itself, able to claim 'as by a soldier's right' the return to the world where

> Over the blackened earth
> The old troops parade,
> Birth heaped on birth
> That such a cannonade
> May thunder time away.[45]

It was this Discord or War that Heraclitus called 'God of all and Father of all, some it has made gods and some men, some bond and some free:' (*A Vision*, p. 67).

18. Blake's illustration of Porphyry's *De Antro Nympharum*, illustrating the cycle of generation. Nymphs are at work with yarn and shuttles, weaving a child (1. foreground) into her 'body of generation'. In the mouth of the river the three Fates draw yarn from a distaff held by a sea-god. The central figure is Odysseus, who is shown in the act of throwing out to sea the 'veil' lent him by the sea-goddess Leucothea. The veiled goddess who points him to the heavenly kingdom of the discarnate is his patron Pallas Athene. Yeats could not have seen this painting, which was discovered at Arlington Court in 1949, and its subject identified by me in the *Warburg Journal* in 1960. See *Blake and Tradition* by Kathleen Raine, Vol. 1, p. 69 et seq.

Yeats's double gyres of *A Vision* run between Concord and Discord, and so will to the end of time. He quotes Simplicius, a late commentator upon Aristotle,

> ... the Concord of Empedocles fabricates all things into "an homogenous sphere", and then Discord separates the elements and so makes the world we inhabit, but even the sphere formed by Concord is not the changeless eternity, for Concord or Love but offers us the image of that which is changeless. (p. 67-8)

And according to Empedocles, 'Never will boundless time be emptied of that pair.'

And this indeed may in part account for Yeats's strange self-identification with those restless heroes who desire not peace but a sword. And yet he was aware of the eternal music, the 'song' which the Shrouds say: 'Now we must sing and sing as best we can.' The singing of souls in a choir is one of the most memorable and beautiful images used by Plotinus, who describes the souls as singing in harmony only when we are turned to the divine Choirmaster. Yeats told Lady Dorothy Wellesley that there were birds which sang like 'linnets' in a choir as if 'taught by a good singing master'.

> They sang, but had nor human tunes nor words
> Though all was done in common as before.
>
> *ll*. 23-24

The 'singing-master' (not mentioned in the poem itself), is again a figure from Plotinus; who writes of the Supreme:

> We are always before it: but we do not always look: thus a choir, singing set in due order about the conductor, may turn away from that centre to which all should attend; let it but face aright and it sings with beauty ... but we do not always attend: when we look, our Term is attained; this is rest; this is the end of singing ill; effectively before Him, we lift a choral song full of God. (VI, 9, 8).

The sages who in 'Sailing to Byzantium' 'perne in a gyre' and are 'the singing-masters' of the soul suggest Plotinus' heavenly choir. In the music there occurs that strange transition from the mortal to the immortal which, like a change of key, resolves the terror of the earlier images into the bird-like lightness Yeats had captured in that line from *The Shadowy Waters*, 'How light we are, now we are changed to birds!'; and from *The Death of Cuchulain*, 'And is it not a strange shape for the soul / Of a great fighting man?' It is in the music itself that the change is modulated — for the music 'had nor human tunes nor words', but belongs to immortality. If the poet, approaching his death, was in truth recalling Plotinus on the divine and very source of poetry, it would indeed be fitting. 'In this choiring, the soul looks upon the wellspring of Life, wellspring also of Intellect, beginning of Being, fount of Good, root of Soul.' (*Ennead*, VI, 9, 9).

The sweet voices of the bird-souls is traditional in the Celtic mythology of the birds, whose unearthly singing is of a beauty described in the written and unwritten tradition of that world; and in Yeats's poems also the bird-voice is the immortal voice; the individual part in the universal harmony; as in the beautiful image of the curlew-cry in an early poem 'Paudeen':

> Until a curlew cried and in the luminous wind
> A curlew answered; and suddenly thereupon I thought
> That on the lonely height where all are in God's eye,
> There cannot be, confusion of our sound forget,
> A single soul that lacks a sweet crystalline cry.
>
> *ll.* 4-8

— or we may recall the hermit who (like Lear in his birdcage?)

> Giddy with his hundredth year
> Sang unnoticed like a bird[46]

— because he had attained in this life the freedom and purity of immortality. 'Thus it is,' according to Plotinus, 'that even in this world the soul which has the desire of the other is putting away, amid its natural life, all that is foreign to that order.'[47]

19. The Gregory Medal of the Irish Academy of Letters by Maurice Lambert (1934). Yeats was responsible for the choice of the artist, and for advising him on the subject and its treatment (the god Aengus and the birds associated with him).

They have changed their throats into the throats of birds. In the play, *The Death of Cuchulain*, the hero's last words, after his sight of his own departing soul as a 'feathery shape' are 'I say it is about to sing': Is it from this music of the liberated soul that the poem takes its title 'Cuchulain Comforted'? Or was his 'comfort' the shroud itself with its secret intimation of rebirth?

'News for the Delphic Oracle' was written a year before 'Cuchulain Comforted'. It tells of that phase of the spirit's cycle of descent and return that Yeats in 'The Soul in Judgment' calls Foreknowledge. For the vision of perfection seen by purified spirits who have rid themselves of the passionate attachments of their former life, those about to return to this world now 'must substitute the next incarnation as fate has decreed it'.[48] Yeats, himself 'content to live it all again', could not in his heart accept Plotinus' 'flight of the alone to the Alone'; and in 'News for the Delphic Oracle' he declares his faith and mocks Plotinus' thought, as in 'The Tower'; and for the same reason, in the name of that wholeness of humanity which is neither life nor death but made up of both phases of the soul's experience.

Plotinus in the fourth *Ennead* has written most fully on the theme that exercised Yeats, of 'how the soul comes to inhabit the body'.

> Many times it has happened; lifted out of the body into myself; becoming external to all other things and self-encentred; beholding a marvellous beauty; then, more than ever, assured of community with the loftiest order; enacting the noblest life, acquiring identity with the divine; stationing within it by having attained that activity; poised above whatsoever within the Intellectual is less than the Supreme: yet, there comes the moment of descent . . . and after that sojourn in the divine, I ask myself how it happens that I can now be descending.

But 'News for the Delphic Oracle' is not written on the soul's descent in general, but specifically on the generation of the hero Achilles; and, by implication, of all those restless and heroic figures who, like Yeats himself, are content 'to live it all again / And yet again'. The iconography of the poem is based (as T. R. Henn has described) upon Nicholas Poussin's 'The Marriage of Thetis and

20. 'The Marriage of Thetis and Peleus' by Nicholas Poussin, 1594-1665. Oil on canvas, 0.97 × 1.35. Lane Bequest, 1918. The National Gallery of Ireland, Dublin. See note on p. 61.

Peleus' in the National Gallery of Dublin. Perhaps the pictorial celebration of that marriage in Dublin gave Yeats another link between Greek Achilles and Irish Cuchulain. The figures of the poem are drawn from both Greek and Irish sources; Plotinus and Pythagoras, Pan, God of nature and lust with his 'foul goathead' (Pan and his goat appear in Poussin's picture); Oisin who, wearied at last of the immortal world and the love of a fairy bride, is drawn back by his longing for earth, is a figure appropriate to the story of the soul's desire for rebirth. Plotinus himself, who appears in the poem, gave Yeats his philosophical structure. He had freely translated 'The

47

Delphic Oracle Upon Plotinus' from Porphyry's *Life*, which tells of the safe arrival of the soul of the philosopher in the Isles of the Blessed:

> Behold that great Plotinus swim,
> Buffeted by such seas;
> Bland Rhadamanthus beckons him,
> But the Golden Race looks dim,
> Salt blood blocks his eyes.
> Scattered on the level grass
> Or winding through the grove
> Plato there and Minos pass,
> There stately Pythagoras
> And all the choir of Love.

Plotinus is described as swimming towards the farther shore of the storm-tossed sea of material existence to the country where Minos and Rhadamanthus are the just rulers of the blessed dead. Yeats had often used the classical image: 'That dolphin-torn, that gong-tormented sea' of 'Byzantium'; the flood whose 'bitter furies of complexity' break on the shores of the Emperor; number iv of the Tarot keys, symbolic monarch of this world. But in 'News for the Delphic Oracle' the ennui of Elysium is suggested with ironic delicacy in terms of the familiar Platonic imagery of a golden race and the Pythagorean harmony:

> There all the golden codgers lay,
> There the silver dew,
> And the great water sighed for love,
> And the wind sighed too.
> Man-picker Niamh leant and sighed
> By Oisin on the grass;
> There sighed amid his choir of love
> Tall Pythagoras.
> Plotinus came and looked about,
> The salt-flakes on his breast,
> And having stretched and yawned awhile
> Lay sighing like the rest.
>
> *ll.* 1-12

Even Plotinus is bored now that the sea's 'ecstatic waters laugh'

> And the brute dolphins plunge
> Until, in some cliff-sheltered bay
> Where wades the choir of love
> Proffering its sacred laurel crowns,
> They pitch their burdens off.
>
> *ll.* 20-24

The dolphins, Hellenic symbol of the vehicles who carry the souls, are described in 'Byzantium' as bearing 'spirit after spirit' to the Emperor's country of 'the unpurged images of day' and 'all complexities of mire and blood'. In the later poem, their burdens are carelessly 'pitched off' upon the farther shore, with a sense of gay and final liberation.

The Delphic Oracle described Plotinus struggling through the sea of material existence to the golden country, his spiritual sight blinded by the physical body.

> Bland Rhadamanthus beckons him,
> But the golden race looks dim,
> Salt blood blocks his eyes.

There is an implicit identification of the salt of blood with the salt of the sea, ancient symbol of material existence and its storms. Conversely, Peleus, in Elysium, about to father Achilles, allows the salt tears of desire to obscure his vision.

> Slim adolescence that a nymph has stripped,
> Peleus on Thetis stares.
> Her limbs are delicate as an eyelid,
> Love has blinded him with tears;
>
> *ll.* 25-28

For him the vision of the golden race will become dimmed; as Blake's Tharmas, his eyes wet with the tears of love tells how '. . all the garden of delight swam like a dream before my eyes.'[49] What subtlety there is in Yeats's beautiful image of Thetis' limbs 'delicate as an eyelid' with the implication that, like salt tears and blood, the sight of her will, like an eyelid, close the spiritual vision of her lover.

Tharmas' line addressed to Enion, weaver of the mortal body, 'Image of grief, thy fading lineaments make my eyelids fail'[50] may have echoed in Yeats's memory. Blake's myth of the 'eternal man' attracted downwards to drown in a living death in the sea of generation is itself based upon a Hermetic myth Yeats must also have known.[51] The resonance of his symbol includes all these tellings of the one mystery.

Plato called this world the cave or grave of the soul, and Plotinus (IV, viii, 3):

> Everywhere we hear of it as in bitter and miserable durance in body, a victim to troubles and desires and fears and all forms of evil, the body its prison or tomb, the Kosmos its cave or cavern.

Yet Plotinus, supreme exemplar of that choice of 'the Supreme', considered the causes of the descent into the cavern:

> Let but the moment arrive and what it decrees will be brought to act by those beings in whom it resides; they fulfill it because they contain it; it prevails because it is within them; it becomes like a heavy burden and sets up in them a painful longing to enter the realm which they are bidden from within. (IV, iii, 14)

The 'leap downward from the Supreme' (IV, iii, 12) is, he says, 'such a leap of the nature as moves men to the instinctive desire of sexual union.' If, as in Plotinus, or in the Tibetan *Book of the Dead* translated by Yeats's friend, Y. Evans-Wentz, the sexual act is envisaged from the side of the discarnate spirit approaching generation it takes on an awe-inspiring, indeed tragic significance. Of this Yeats was deeply aware; already in *Responsibilities* (1914) he had seen the Magi

> ... their eyes still fixed, hoping to find once more,
> Being by Calvary's turbulence unsatisfied,
> The uncontrollable mystery on the bestial floor.[52]

In 'Leda and the Swan' these tragic implications are explicit:

> A shudder in the loins engenders there
> The broken wall, the burning roof and tower
> And Agamemnon dead.
>
> *ll.* 9-11

— the destructive work of the hero Achilles. In 'News for the Delphic Oracle' sexual desire draws towards generation the soul of Achilles, whose birth is implicit in the naming of his parents.

> ... Thetis' belly listens.
> Down the mountain walls
> From where Pan's cavern is
> Intolerable music falls.
>
> *ll.* 29-32

In an earlier poem, 'Among Schoolchildren', it is the 'honey of generation' which 'betrays' the soul into birth. In this poem Yeats was thinking of the honeyed cup of Porphyry's 'Cave of the Nymphs' which the souls falling into generation drink as they are about to enter the Zodiac of time from the sphere of eternity. He had read this work many years before, and in his early essay on 'The Philosophy of Shelley's Poetry' recalls 'the cold intoxicating cup, given to the souls in the constellation of the Cup near the constellation Cancer.' There is, in Thomas Taylor's translation of this work (doubtless Yeats's source of this knowledge) a note to the effect that 'honey' is in the context symbolic of sexual desire; instancing the myth of the ensnaring of Saturn by making the god drunk with a honeyed drink.

The celestial music of the Choir of Love, the 'sweet and strange' bird-voices of the soul (which we may trace from the human-headed bird-souls of *The Shadowy Waters* whose 'strange cries' draw Forgael away from the mortal world), have their antithesis in the 'intolerable music' from 'Pan's cavern' which draws the soul downwards into generation in the Platonic Cave. Both Plato and Pythagoras make a distinction between music which raises and purifies the soul, and music which arouses the lower instincts and passions. In *The Republic* the Lydian and Myxolydian modes were to be forbidden; for Socrates in that dialogue says that corruption enters a society above all through its music.

I may be mistaken — for Yeats was so widely and variously learned in these themes — in discerning in the 'intolerable music' from Pan's cavern an echo also from Evan-Wentz's translation of the account in the Tibetan *Bardo Thodol* of the attraction of disembodied souls towards rebirth. Among these downward attractions are hallucinations of various kinds including 'rock caverns, deep holes in the earth' and also 'songs like wailings, due to evil karma',[53] will be heard. The irresistable attraction towards rebirth is also said to come about through 'visions of mating men and women'. 'To every soul its own hour; when that strikes it descends and enters the body suitable to it.' Plotinus himself speaks of the impulse 'set stirring and advancing as by a mighty traction . . . stirring and bringing forth, in due season, every element — beard, horn.' (IV, iii, 14). We may wonder if this very phrase, with its strangely (for Plotinus) animal images, fusing in the poet's thought, perhaps, with the more horrific phantasmagoria of the Tibetan *Bardo*, enter into the concluding image of his poem, with its evocation, in triumphant acceptance of the impulse towards generation, of Poussin's 'Marriage of Peleus and Thetis'.

> Foul goathead, brutal arm appear,
> Belly, shoulder, bum,
> Flash fish-like, nymphs and satyrs
> Copulate in the foam,
> In the waters of the sea, universal symbol of generation.
>
> *ll.* 33-36

21. Detail of Plate 20 : The Marriage of Thetis and Peleus by Nicholas Proussin.

It is not my intention to argue the claims of the traditional gnosis which I have indicated as the very substance of Yeats's inspiration, first and last. He himself, in an early essay, invoked William Blake, who wrote: 'When I tell any truth it is not for the sake of convincing those who do not know it, but for the sake of defending those who do.' Such claims, in any case, cannot be argued. Yeats, like Blake, made his appeal to knowledge, not to credence; a knowledge which has its learned books but which is also innate in us, which causes us to respond to his great symbols, whatever with our conscious minds we may believe or disbelieve. If indeed the soul is, as Yeats and his teachers tell us, an immortal migrant, how immeasurably greater is the human being and the human destiny, as Yeats seeks to disclose it to us, than the momentary and spectral existence of mortality? In this 'mysterious wisdom won by toil' this vast self-knowledge, this revelation of life, death and immortality as one single unbroken journey, Yeats has restored to us a lost universe of experience the scholar in his tower has yet scarcely begun to realize:

> Just truth enough to show that his whole life
> Will scarcely find for him a broken crust
> Of all those truths that are your daily bread;[53]

## NOTE ON *THE DEATH OF CUCHULAIN*

The theme of the veil as an ambiguous symbol of the beautiful incarnate body, and of the shroud, has in this play yet another probable association. For what follows I am indebted to Mr. Liam Miller, who has thought deeply about the play from the point of view of stage-production. (*The Death of Cuchulain*, directed and with stage designs by Liam Miller, was produced in January 1972 at the Lantern Theatre in Dublin.)

If Mr. Miller is right (and here the man of the theatre is more likely to be right than academic writers who have put forward other views) the prologue to this play is not only Yeats's own dramatic testament, but a final tribute to Edward Gordon Craig, to whom he was indebted for ideas and techniques which, from 1900 to 1920 he himself attempted to put into practise.

It seems that the words of the Old Man who speaks the Prologue, 'unless indeed I am, as I affirm, the son of Talma' may point to Gordon Craig, who was the natural son of Ellen Terry. If the speaker be Craig, his words 'I wrote certain guiding principles' would refer to Edward Gordon Craig's *On the Art of the Theatre* and his other critical works on the Theatre. The whole speech can be related to Craig's writings; both to his principles — not pandering to the audience, etc. — and to his techniques. Gordon Craig was Yeats's first mask-maker; and Yeats had designed sets using Craig's system at the Abbey Theatre from 1910 on. Yeats's first attempt at Gordon Craig's stylised system, the set for Lady Gregory's *The Deliverer*, was compared by Joseph Holloway to children's building-blocks. The speaker of the Prologue answers such criticism when he asks for formalised heads because 'no wood carving can look so well as a parallelogram of painted wood.' (In Liam Miller's production the pillar stone to which Cuchulain is bound is made up of the same blocks of wood as later serve as the 'heads' — an economy of 'props' comparable with that of the Noh stage, Yeats's other precedent for his formal stylization.)

The dancer of whom the Prologue speaks cannot be Ninette de Valois, who by 1939 was already setting Dégas-like dancers in motion in the Sadlers Wells Ballet; for the Old Man says, 'I spit upon the dancers painted by Dégas. I spit upon their short bodies, their stiff stays, their toes whereon they spin like peg-tops. . . .' Gordon Craig's dancer would have been Isadora Duncan: 'I could have got such a dancer once, but she has gone: the tragi-comedian dancer, the tragic dancer, upon the same neck love and loathing, life and death.' Isadora's death was caused by her long floating scarf (characteristic of her dress and style as a dancer) being caught around her neck in a motoring accident. So perhaps the winding of Aoife's veil around the dying hero, its unwinding by the Blind Man ('. . . some womanish stuff') while on one level symbolic, takes an added force of tragic meaning from the death of so great an artist of the dance as Yeats and Gordon Craig conceived it.

The mood of the play is bitter; the dying hero's head cut off by the Blind Man for the offered reward of 'twelve pennies', reflecting perhaps Yeats's sense not only of the betrayal of the Irish revolution by her own begetters, but perhaps also his own sense of betrayal by his own creature, the Irish National Theatre. If the concluding song, 'The harlot sang to the beggar-man' carries an echo of Blake's

> The harlot's cry from street to street
> Shall weave old England's winding-sheet

(shrouds again) the bitter voice of the prologue is echoed in the close.

The 'triple death' of Cuchulain — from his wounds, from Aoife, and from the Blind Man — is a theme associated with many of Ireland's half-legendary kings. (See *Irish Kings and High Kings* by Francis John Byrne, Batsford 1973.)

## NOTES

1 'Some Contemporary Poets', *Science and Poetry*, 1927.
2 'The Later Poetry of W. B. Yeats', *Southern Review*, 1936. Reprinted in *Form and Value in Modern Poetry*, 1957.
3 *Troades* II. vi. 9.
4 *Gorgias* 492d, trans. by W. D. Woodhead.
5 *Letters of W. B. Yeats*, p. 370.
6 Trans. Hugh Tredennick, 71 d-e.
7 *Op. cit.*, 67e-68a.
8 *Op. cit.*, 71c.
9 'Blood and the Moon', *Collected Poems*, p. 269, II, 7-11.
10 *Op. cit.*, 72e.
11 Letter to John Flaxman, 21 September 1800. *Complete Writings*, ed. Geoffrey Keynes, p. 801.
12 Monk Gibbon, *The Masterpiece and the Man* (1959), p. 53.
13 'On Swedenborg, Mediums and the Desolate Places.' Appendix to Lady Gregory's *Visions and Beliefs*, Vol. II (1920), p. 306.
14 *Op. cit.*, pp. 296-297.
15 *Op. cit.*, p. 303.
16 *Op. cit.*, p. 301.
17 *Op. cit.*, pp. 302-303.
18 *Op. cit.*, p. 322.
19 *Op. cit.*, p. 303.
20 *Op. cit.*, p. 333-337.
21 *A Vision*, p. 231.
22 *Ennead*, IV.viii.4.
23 *Ennead*, VI. ix. 11.
24 *Ennead*, IV.viii.4v.
25 *Ennead*, IV.viii.5.
26 W. B. Yeats, *Letters on Poetry to Dorothy Wellesley*, Oxford University Press, 1940, pp. 212-213.
27 The poem 'Hercules and Meleager' (No. 308 of the *Oxford Book of Greek Verse*, edited by his friend Maurice Bowra, and appearing in 1938) may have reminded Yeats of a theme long important to him. I am indebted to Professor Francis Byrne for this suggestion.
28 *Op. cit.*, pp. 338-339.
29 *Collected Poems*, pp. 483484.
30 *A Vision*, p. 226.
31 *Ennead*, IV.iii.27.
32 *Op. cit.*, p. 338.
33 *Ennead*, IV.iii.32.
34 Another source of the heads may be Blake's design for Gray's 'The Fatal

Sisters', and that poem itself, whose theme is taken from Irish history. Gray's poem is a paraphrase of an Icelandic poem of the eleventh century entitled 'Darraz ar Lióz', or 'Lay of Darts'. It refers to the battle of Clontarf, which was fought on Good Friday 1014. I here quote Gray's preface:

> In the Eleventh century, Sigurd, Earl of the Orkney-Islands went with a fleet of ships and a considerable body of troops into Ireland, to the assistance of *Sictryg with the Silken beard*, who was then making war on his father-in-law *Brian*, King of Dublin: The Earl and all his forces were cut to pieces, and *Sictryg* was in danger of a total defeat; but the enemy had a greater loss by the death of *Brian*, their King, who fell in the action. On Christmas-day, (the day of the battle), a native of *Caithness* in Scotland saw at a distance a number of persons on horseback riding full speed towards the hill, and seeming to enter into it. Curiosity led him to follow them, till looking through the opening in the rocks he saw twelve gigantic figures resembling women: they were all employed about a loom; and as they wove, they sang the following dreadful song; which when they had finished, they tore the web into twelve pieces, and (each taking her portion) galloped Six to the North and as many to the South.

Gray has in his poem captured something of the primitive power of this symbol of the weaving of the woof of death by the Valkyries; and it is tempting to imagine that Yeats's imagination had been at some time captured by the poem and Blake's grisly illustration of the lines:

> See the griesly texture grow %
> ('Tis of human entrails made)
> And the weights, that play below,
> Each a gasping Warriour's head.

There is no more impressive account of the Valkyries in English poetry; and there are lines referring to Brian, king of Dublin, which might equally have been related of Cuchulain himself:

> Low the dauntless Earl is laid,
> Gor'd with many a gaping wound:
> Fate demands a nobler head;
> Soon a King shall bite the ground.
>
> Long his loss shall Erin weep,
> Ne'er again his likeness see;
> Long her strains in sorrow steep,
> Strains of Immortality!

This is of course pure speculation; but the mood of Emer's 'tragic joy' is not unlike the primitive battle-joy captured by Gray in this ancient poem.

35  *A Vision*, p. 197.
36  *The Divine Pymander*, trans. Everard, Book VIII, 7-8.
37  *A Vision*, pp. 232-233.
38  Blake was himself drawing upon a Hermetic myth no doubt known to Yeats either from Everard's seventeenth century translation, (which Blake knew), *The Divine Pymander of Hermes Trismegistus*, or from G. R. S. Meade's *Thrice Greatest Hermes* (1906). In the Second Book (called the 'Poemander') the archetypal man made in the 'Form or Shape of God', sees his own reflection in the material element symbolically called 'water';

> which when he saw . . . he Smiled for love, as if he had seen the Shape or Likeness in the Water, or the Shadow upon Earth of the fairest Human form. And seeing in the Water a shape, a shape like unto himself he loved it, and would cohabit with it; and immediately upon the resolution, ensued the Operation. . . . (Trans. Everard, 1650.) So it is (the Poemander continues) that Man above all things that live upon Earth is double; Mortal because of his Body, and Immortal because of the substantial man.

This is the story Blake retells in the horrific account of the drowning of Tharmas in the 'sea' of matter by Enion, the feminine material principle. See *Blake and the Tradition*, Kathleen Raine, Vol. I, p. 271 *et seq.*

39  'A Vision of the Last Judgment', *Blake's Complete Writings*, ed. Keynes, p. 607. Modern spiritualists — notably Raynor C. Johnson — also write of these composite or group-souls.
40  *A Vision*, p. 234.
41  *A Vision*, 'The Soul in Judgment', p. 237.
42  Trans. Paul Shorey. Xc.
43  'The Phases of the Moon', p. 187.
44  'A Dialogue of Self and Soul', *ll.* 57-60.
45  'Mohini Chatterjee', *ll.* 21-25.
46  'The Three Hermits', *ll.* 6-7.
47  *Ennead*, IV.iii.32.
48  *A Vision*, p. 234.
49  'Vala' Night the Third, l.195, Keynes, p. 297.
50  'Vala' Night the Seventh, (b) 235, Keynes, p. 339.
51  *Hermetica* II, the 'Poemander', 18-26.
52  'The Magi', *ll.* 6-8.
53  The Tibetan *Book of the Dead*, XL, p. 185.
54  'The Phases of the Moon', *ll.* 24-26.

## ACKNOWLEDGEMENTS

First I wish to thank Miss Anne Yeats and Senator Michael Yeats for permission to quote the poems *Cuchulain Comforted* and *News for the Delphic Oracle*, and other passages from Yeats's writings quoted in this book; and for their generosity in allowing me access to Yeats's library, and to unpublished manuscripts. I also wish to thank Princeton University Press and Mr. William MacGuire, general editor of the Bollingen Series, for kindly supplying me with photographs of some plates made by them for my *Blake and Tradition* (Bollingen Series, 1968, Andrew Mellon Lectures 1962). To Mr. Liam Miller also my thanks for allowing the photograph of his mask for the Morrigu in *The Death of Cuchulain* to be included.

## LIST OF ILLUSTRATIONS

Cover and p. 5   1. The 'veiled' Goddess: Juno Samia Selenitis; engraving from Jacob Bryant's *New System of Mythology*, Vol. 2 (1774), plate vii.

p. 13   2. The thirteenth Tarot key: Death. From *The Twenty-two Keys of the Tarot* by Arland Ussher, Dublin, 1957.

p. 25   3. Cuchulain: Statue by Oliver Sheppard in the General Post Office, Dublin. The Morrigu in bird-form is perched above the head of the hero; who is bound with the 'veil', as described by Yeats in *The Death of Cuchulain*.

p. 26   4. The Morrigu. Mask designed by Liam Miller and Hugh Kearns for a production at the Lantern Theatre, Dublin, 1972.

p. 27   5. Cloth by Edmund Dulac for the first production of *At the Hawk's Well*, 1916.

p. 30   6. John Donne's monument in St. Paul's Cathedral, London. This sculpture, with its suggestion at once of death and resurrection, was made according to the poet's own instructions, he himself standing in his shroud to serve as the model of his own effigy.

p. 31   7. Blake: The worm (Blake's customary symbol of the mortal body) in her winding-sheet, in 'the regions of the grave'. *The Gates of Paradise*, plate 16.

p. 32   8. Blake: The generated soul woven into the 'filmy Woof'. *Jerusalem* (1804-1820) plate 37, detail.

p. 34   9. Blake: Vala (veiled) mother of mortal bodies, and Jerusalem (nude) mother of souls. *Jerusalem*, plate 32.

p. 35   10. *The Bride* by William Calvert. This line engraving by one of that group of younger artists who took Blake as their master, is within the iconographic tradition of the 'veiled' goddess from which Blake himself derived, and which he transmitted. Yeats greatly admired this engraving.

p. 36   11. Blake: Design (early 1790's) for Gray's *The Fatal Sisters*.

p. 38   12. Blake: Daughters of Los (Time) at the Wheel, spinning the 'fibres of life'.

p. 39   13. The thread of Fate: detail from Blake's water-colour drawing illustrating Gray's *Ode on the Death of a Favourite Cat*. See also Plate no.

p. 39   14. Blake: The Blessed Virgin Mary drawing yarn from a distaff: Illustration (c. 1816) to Milton's *Paradise Regained*.

p. 39   15. The Blessed Virgin Mary with spinning-wheel and distaff: detail from illustration to the *Divine Comedy* (1827), No. 3. In these two depictions of the symbolism of generation, Blake indicates that through the Christian Mystery of the Incarnation the 'body of death' is redeemed.

p. 41   16. Blake: *The Gates of Paradise*, Frontispiece (1793). The crysalis with the face of a sleeping infant suggests at once the unborn child about to enter this life; and the 'body of death' awaiting metamorphosis. Was Blake's image suggested by some such Tudor effigy as that of

p. 41   17. Robert Clayton, in St. Giles's Church, Ickenham, Middlesex, 'who dyed 16th of August 1665 within a few howres after his birth'

(This effigy was reproduced on the title-page of a volume of poems by Frances Bellerby, published by the Enitharmon Press, London, 1970; to whom, and to Mrs. Bellerby, acknowledgements are made.)

p. 43   18. Blake's illustration of Porphyry's *De Antro Nympharum*, illustrating the cycle of generation. Nymphs are at work with yarn and shuttles, weaving a child (l. foreground) into her 'body of generation'. In the mouth of the river the three Fates drew yarn from a distaff held by a sea-god. The central figure is Odysseus, who is shown in the act of throwing out to sea the 'veil' lent him by the sea-goddess Leucothea. The veiled goddess who points him to the heavenly kingdom of the discarnate is his patron Pallas Athene. Yeats could not have seen this painting, which was discovered at Arlington Court in 1949, and its subject identified by me in the *Warburg Journal* in 1960. See *Blake and Tradition* (1968) by Kathleen Raine, Vol. 1, p. 69 *et seq*.

p. 45   19. The Gregory Medal of the Irish Academy of Letters by Maurice Lambert (1934). Yeats was responsible for the choice of the artist, and for advising him on the subject and its treatment (the god Aengus and the birds associated with him).

p. 47   20. 'The Marriage of Thetis and Peleus' by Nicholas Poussin. The following extract is taken from the catalogue of the Yeats Centenary Exhibition, 1965, in the National Gallery of Ireland, Dublin:

Formerly exhibited as *Acis and Galatea*. *Thetis*, the daughter of Nereus, was sought in marriage by Zeus and Neptune, but she bestowed her hand upon Peleus, a mortal. Her marriage was attended by the gods and her sister Nereids. A drawing of part of the composition by Poussin is in the Gallery, No. 2769. Yeats was inspired by the mythology portrayed in this painting when he wrote "News for the Delphic Oracle". By Nicholas Poussin, 1594-1665. Oil on canvas, 0.97 × 1.35. Lane Bequest, 1918.

According to *Nicholas Poussin* by Thomas MacGreevy, Dublin 1960, the earlier attribution (*Acis and Galatea*) is the correct one.